Keep in mind...
If you put forth 1/2 the effort, you only get a fraction of the results.

Simplifying Fractions

I. Numerator Smaller than Denominator

$$\frac{4 \div 4}{8 \div 4} \quad \text{(greatest common factor)} = \frac{1}{2}$$

1. $\dfrac{6}{9}$

2. $\dfrac{10}{25}$

3. $\dfrac{7}{14}$

4. $\dfrac{8}{24}$

5. $\dfrac{36}{60}$

6. $\dfrac{18}{36}$

7. $\dfrac{8}{28}$

8. $\dfrac{21}{45}$

9. $\dfrac{12}{40}$

10. $\dfrac{19}{57}$

11. $\dfrac{20}{28}$

12. $\dfrac{18}{44}$

0-88012-866-6

...More Simplifying

II. Numerator larger than denominator

$$\frac{12 \div 3}{9 \div 3} = \frac{4}{3}$$

Improper Fraction

$$\frac{12 \div 3}{9 \div 3} = \frac{4}{3} = \frac{3}{3} + \frac{1}{3} = 1 + \frac{1}{3} = 1\frac{1}{3}$$

Mixed Numeral

Write answers as improper fractions.

1. $\dfrac{15}{6}$

2. $\dfrac{36}{27}$

3. $\dfrac{40}{14}$

4. $\dfrac{20}{12}$

5. $\dfrac{52}{28}$

6. $\dfrac{33}{27}$

7. $\dfrac{28}{24}$

8. $\dfrac{66}{27}$

Now go back and write the answers as mixed numerals.

Adding and Subtracting Fractions

I. Like Denominators

$$\frac{\overset{\text{add}}{\frown}}{1}{8} + \frac{3}{8} = \frac{4}{8} = \frac{1}{2}$$

same

1. $\dfrac{2}{9} + \dfrac{5}{9}$

2. $\dfrac{3}{4} - \dfrac{1}{4}$

3. $\dfrac{9}{15} + \dfrac{5}{15}$

4. $\dfrac{19}{20} - \dfrac{14}{20}$

5. $\dfrac{27}{38} + \dfrac{13}{38}$

6. $\dfrac{35}{60} - \dfrac{17}{60}$

7. $\dfrac{17}{20} + \dfrac{23}{20}$

8. $\dfrac{25}{13} - \dfrac{12}{13}$

9. $\dfrac{11}{18} + \dfrac{16}{18}$

10. $\dfrac{17}{48} - \dfrac{14}{48}$

11. $\dfrac{7}{45} + \dfrac{8}{45}$

12. $\dfrac{33}{50} - \dfrac{17}{50}$

0-88012-866-6

...More Adding and Subtracting

II. Unlike Denominators

$$\frac{7}{9} - \frac{1}{4} = \frac{28}{36} - \frac{9}{36} = \frac{19}{36}$$

36 is the
least common
multiple

1. $\dfrac{2}{3} + \dfrac{5}{9}$

2. $\dfrac{4}{5} - \dfrac{3}{4}$

3. $\dfrac{5}{6} + \dfrac{7}{12}$

4. $\dfrac{11}{15} - \dfrac{2}{5}$

5. $\dfrac{11}{12} + \dfrac{5}{8}$

6. $\dfrac{1}{2} - \dfrac{4}{9}$

7. $\dfrac{13}{36} + \dfrac{5}{12}$

8. $\dfrac{7}{8} - \dfrac{3}{10}$

9. $\dfrac{4}{9} + \dfrac{13}{15}$

10. $\dfrac{5}{12} - \dfrac{5}{18}$

11. $\dfrac{5}{9} + \dfrac{3}{8}$

12. $\dfrac{5}{12} - \dfrac{3}{15}$

...And More Adding and Subtracting

III. Mixed Numerals

$$3\frac{7}{8} + 5\frac{11}{24} = 3\frac{21}{24} + 5\frac{11}{24} = 8\frac{32}{24} = 9\frac{8}{24} = 9\frac{1}{3}$$

(add / add)

1. $1\frac{1}{4} + 2\frac{1}{2}$

2. $5\frac{7}{10} - 1\frac{1}{6}$

3. $8\frac{3}{8} + 9\frac{2}{3}$

4. $6 - 2\frac{8}{11}$

5. $2\frac{1}{16} + 2\frac{1}{3}$

6. $7\frac{7}{8} - 7\frac{5}{12}$

7. $4\frac{1}{2} + 6\frac{2}{5}$

8. $5\frac{1}{2} - \frac{11}{15}$

9. $1\frac{5}{6} + 4$

10. $6\frac{7}{9} - 6\frac{1}{2}$

11. $7\frac{1}{4} + 1\frac{7}{9} + 2\frac{5}{6}$

12. $8\frac{1}{6} - 7\frac{3}{4}$

0-88012-866-6

Multiplying Fractions

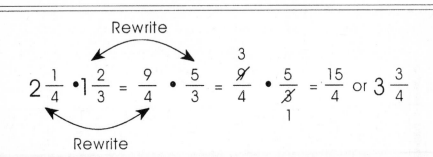

1. $\dfrac{1}{2} \cdot \dfrac{5}{6}$

2. $3 \cdot \dfrac{1}{2}$

3. $\dfrac{2}{5} \cdot \dfrac{1}{3}$

4. $\dfrac{16}{5} \cdot \dfrac{25}{27}$

5. $\dfrac{8}{21} \cdot 2\dfrac{7}{16}$

6. $1\dfrac{5}{7} \cdot 2\dfrac{1}{4}$

7. $5\dfrac{7}{8} \cdot 4$

8. $\dfrac{5}{7} \cdot \dfrac{7}{5}$

9. $3\dfrac{2}{3} \cdot \dfrac{17}{22}$

10. $\dfrac{1}{2} \cdot \dfrac{6}{11} \cdot \dfrac{3}{5}$

11. $9\dfrac{1}{3} \cdot 1\dfrac{5}{7} \cdot \dfrac{3}{4}$

12. $2\dfrac{1}{4} \cdot 6 \cdot 1\dfrac{1}{9}$

0-88012-866-6

Dividing Fractions

$$1\frac{1}{2} \div 3\frac{3}{7} = \frac{3}{2} \div \frac{24}{7} = \frac{3}{2} \cdot \frac{7}{24} = \frac{\cancel{3}}{2} \cdot \frac{7}{\cancel{24}_8} = \frac{7}{16}$$

Invert and Multiply

Rewrite

1. $\dfrac{3}{7} \div \dfrac{1}{2}$

2. $\dfrac{17}{9} \div \dfrac{8}{9}$

3. $6\dfrac{2}{3} \div 5$

4. $1\dfrac{7}{9} \div 4\dfrac{2}{9}$

5. $\dfrac{15}{4} \div \dfrac{5}{14}$

6. $\dfrac{11}{12} \div \dfrac{13}{8}$

7. $4 \div 4\dfrac{2}{5}$

8. $3\dfrac{1}{4} \div 4\dfrac{3}{8}$

9. $\dfrac{6}{15} \div \dfrac{9}{10}$

10. $\dfrac{7}{8} \div 2\dfrac{1}{3}$

11. $9\dfrac{3}{8} \div 3\dfrac{3}{4}$

12. $5\dfrac{1}{6} \div \dfrac{31}{6}$

0-88012-866-6

Mixed Practice with Fractions

1. $1\frac{1}{3} + \frac{5}{6}$

2. $\frac{4}{7} \cdot \frac{11}{16}$

3. $5 \div 6\frac{1}{4}$

4. $\frac{11}{17} + \frac{15}{17}$

5. $7\frac{2}{5} - 2\frac{1}{4}$

6. $2\frac{2}{3} \cdot 3\frac{3}{5}$

7. $2\frac{4}{7} \div \frac{20}{21}$

8. $\frac{42}{11} - \frac{7}{2}$

9. $\frac{5}{12} + \frac{7}{24} + \frac{31}{26}$

10. $\frac{13}{25} \cdot \frac{10}{39} \cdot \frac{15}{2}$

11. $6\frac{1}{4} - 3\frac{2}{3}$

12. $\frac{7}{2} \div \frac{5}{3}$

13. $8\frac{1}{3} + 2\frac{3}{10}$

14. $11\frac{1}{6} - \frac{5}{9}$

15. $\frac{2}{13} \cdot 3\frac{5}{7} \cdot 4\frac{1}{2}$

16. $5\frac{2}{3} \div 1\frac{2}{15}$

17. $4\frac{1}{8} + 2\frac{6}{16} - 6\frac{1}{2}$

18. $\left(1\frac{5}{9} \cdot 3\right) \div \frac{1}{3}$

19. $1\frac{4}{5} + 1\frac{1}{6} + 1\frac{1}{30}$

20. $\frac{7}{9} + \left(\frac{11}{12} \div \frac{33}{8}\right)$

8

0-88012-866-6

Problems with Fractions

1. If $1\frac{1}{4}$ pounds of bananas sell for 80¢ and $1\frac{1}{3}$ pounds of apples sell for 90¢, which fruit is cheaper?

2. A cake recipe calls for $\frac{2}{3}$ teaspoon salt, $1\frac{1}{2}$ teaspoons baking powder, 1 teaspoon baking soda and $\frac{1}{2}$ teaspoon cinnamon. How many total teaspoons of dry ingredients are used?

3. A baseball team played 35 games and won $\frac{4}{7}$ of them.
   How many games were won?
   How many games were lost?

4. During 4 days, the price of the stock of PEV Corporation went up $\frac{1}{4}$ of a point, down $\frac{1}{3}$ of a point, down $\frac{3}{4}$ of a point and up $\frac{7}{10}$ of a point. What was the net change?

 0-88012-866-6

Changing Fractions to Decimals

$$\frac{7}{20} \Rightarrow 20\overline{\smash{\big)}\,7.00} \Rightarrow \frac{7}{20} = .35$$

terminating

$$\frac{5}{12} \Rightarrow 12\overline{\smash{\big)}\,5.00000} \Rightarrow \frac{5}{12} = .41\overline{6}$$

repeating

1. $\dfrac{3}{5}$

2. $\dfrac{11}{25}$

3. $\dfrac{7}{15}$

4. $2\dfrac{1}{9}$

5. $\dfrac{23}{33}$

6. $1\dfrac{5}{16}$

 0-88012-866-6

 Keep in mind...
Don't wait for things to be just right before you get started. Start now!

Rounding Decimals

Round 8.135 to the nearest tenth.
8.1<u>3</u>5 ⟹ 8.1
‿
less than 5

Round 32.56713 to the nearest hundredth.
32.56<u>7</u>13 ⟹ 32.57
‿
greater than 5

ound to the nearest whole number.

1. 41.803　　　2. 119.63　　　3. 20.05　　　4. 3.45

ound to the nearest tenth.

5. 33.335　　　6. 1.861　　　7. 99.96　　　8. 103.103

?ound to the nearest hundredth.

9. 69.713　　　10. 5.569　　　11. 609.906　　　12. 247.898

Multiplying and Dividing by 10, 100, etc.

$$34.61 \times 1\underline{0} \Rightarrow 34.61 \Rightarrow 346.1$$

move right

$$6.77 \times 1\underline{00} \Rightarrow 6.77 \Rightarrow 677$$

$$105.61 \div 1,\underline{000} \Rightarrow 105.61 \Rightarrow .10561$$

move left

1. 4.81 x 100

2. 37.68 ÷ 10

3. .46 x 1,000

4. 7.12 ÷ 10,000

5. 5.4 x 10

6. 27,500 ÷ 1,000

7. 4.395 x 100,000

8. .0075 ÷ 100

9. 2.274 x 10

10. 90,000 ÷ 100

11. .000618 x 1,000

12. 39.006 ÷ 1,000

12 0-88012-866-6

Adding and Subtracting Decimals

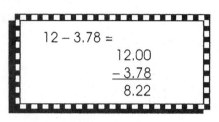

12 − 3.78 =

$$12.00$$
$$-\ 3.78$$
$$8.22$$

. 3.5 + 8.4

7. 7.6 + 12.412

. 17.6 − 9.3

8. 83.06 − 12.3

. 43.57 + 104.6

9. 2.304 + 6.18 + 9.2

. 21.3 − 16.5

10. 291.36 − 187.837

. 15.36 + 29.23 - 7.2

11. $12.91 + $6.99

. 32.3 − 12.72

12. 5.25 + 23.96 − 19.931

Multiplying Decimals

$$(.7) (.04) = \begin{array}{r} .7 \\ \underline{\times .04} \\ .028 \end{array}$$

3 decimal places

3 decimal places

1. (.003) (6)

6. (5.29) (11.3)

2. (.051) (.003)

7. (.017) (6.2)

3. (260) (.01)

8. (.3) (.03) (.003)

4. (9.6) (5)

9. (.05) (.16) (.001)

5. (7) (3.42)

10. (8) (.217) (.01)

---

14 0-88012-866-6

Dividing Decimals

$$.03652 \div .88 = \quad .88.\overline{)\,.036520}$$

```
            .0415
  .88.).036520
        352
        132
         88
        440
        440
          0
```

1. $.128 \div .8$

2. $2.45 \div 3.5$

3. $.5773 \div 5.02$

4. $39.78 \div .195$

5. $4.2016 \div 5.2$

0-88012-866-6

Mixed Practice with Decimals

1. 12.16 − 8.72

2. 119.7 + 11.97

3. (3.4) (8)

4. 2960 ÷ .37

5. 1.21 ÷ 1.1

6. 7 + 6.91

7. 18.91 − 11.857

8. (1.35) (21.4)

9. 21.2 − 9.03

10. .7 + .02 + 4

11. (.25) (2.5) (25)

12. 95.6 − 87.81 + 12.21

 0-88012-866-6

Problems with Decimals

1. Jim's gas credit card bill was $80.97 for June, $41.35 for July and $65.08 for August. What were his total charges for the summer?

2. One cup of hot chocolate can be made with .18 ounces of hot chocolate mix. How many cups can be made from a 6.48 ounce canister of mix?

3. Karl's car payments are $215.37 per month for the next three years. What will be the total amount he will pay for his car?

4. The dress Sally wants costs $85.15. If the price was reduced by $12.78, how much will she pay?

More Changing Fractions to Decimals

1. $\dfrac{3}{8}$

2. $\dfrac{8}{15}$

3. $\dfrac{27}{32}$

4. $\dfrac{23}{30}$

5. $\dfrac{4}{7}$

6. $5\dfrac{1}{8}$

7. $1\dfrac{4}{5}$

8. $\dfrac{10}{35}$

9. $\dfrac{9}{15}$

10. $2\dfrac{3}{8}$

0-88012-866-6

Changing Decimals to Fractions

Terminating Decimals

$$.25 = \frac{25}{100} = \frac{1}{4}$$

$$.132 = \frac{132}{1000} = \frac{33}{250}$$

Repeating Decimals

$$N = .\overline{12} = .121212\ldots$$

$$1\underline{00}N = 12.1212\ldots$$

$$- \quad N = - .1212\ldots$$

$$\frac{99N}{99} = \frac{12}{99}$$

$$N = \frac{4}{33}$$

$$\text{or } .\overline{12} = \frac{4}{33}$$

1. .125

2. $.\overline{6}$

3. .36

4. $.\overline{46}$

5. .6875

19
0-88012-866-6

Keep in mind...
**Life is 10% what you make it
and 90% how you take it.**

Ratios and Proportions

I. Write each ratio as a fraction in simplest form.

$$3 \text{ to } 12 \Rightarrow \frac{3}{12} = \frac{1}{4} \qquad\qquad 65 : 35 \Rightarrow \frac{65}{35} = \frac{13}{7}$$

$$6 \text{ out of } 40 \Rightarrow \frac{6}{40} = \frac{3}{20}$$

1. 196 to 7   3. 18 out of 27   5. .11 : 1.21

2. 19 : 76   4. $\frac{3}{8}$ to $\frac{3}{4}$ 6. 140 : 112

II. Solve each proportion.

$$\frac{3}{7} = \frac{x}{49}$$
$$3 \cdot 49 = 7x$$
$$\frac{147}{7} = \frac{7x}{7}$$
$$21 = x$$

1. $\dfrac{8}{6} = \dfrac{m}{27}$ 4. $\dfrac{9}{p} = \dfrac{5}{2}$

2. $\dfrac{z}{3} = \dfrac{8}{15}$ 5. $\dfrac{1.8}{x} = \dfrac{3.6}{2.4}$

3. $\dfrac{16}{40} = \dfrac{24}{c}$ 6. $\dfrac{4}{5} = \dfrac{.8}{y}$

Problems Using Proportions

Three loaves of bread cost $3.87.
How much do 2 loaves cost?

$$\frac{\text{number of loaves}}{\text{cost}}$$

$$\frac{3}{3.87} = \frac{2}{x}$$

$$3x = 2 \cdot 3.87$$

$$\frac{3x}{3} = \frac{7.74}{3}$$

$$x = 2.58$$

2 loaves cost $2.58.

1. If 64 feet of rope weigh 20 pounds, how much will 80 feet of the same type of rope weigh?

2. If a 10 pound turkey takes four hours to cook, how long will it take a 14 pound turkey to cook?

3. An 18 ounce box of cereal costs $2.76. How many ounces should a box priced at $2.07 contain?

4. Mike and Pat traveled 392 miles in seven hours. If they travel at the same rate, how long will it take them to travel 728 miles?

0-88012-866-6

Percents

Write each expression as a percent.

$$\frac{3}{4} \Rightarrow \frac{3}{4} = \frac{x}{100}$$
$$300 = 4x$$
$$75 = x$$
$$\frac{3}{4} = 75\%$$

$$.375 \Rightarrow .375 = 37.5\%$$

Move decimal
2 places to the
right.

1. $\frac{4}{5}$

4. 2.5

7. 1.125

2. $\frac{4}{7}$

5. $\frac{3}{8}$

8. $\frac{1}{2}$

3. .22

6. .006

9. $\frac{9}{40}$

Write each percent as a fraction.

$$90\%$$
$$90\% = \frac{90}{100} = \frac{9}{10}$$

$$61.5\%$$
$$61.5\% = \frac{61.5}{100} = \frac{615}{1000} = \frac{123}{200}$$

1. 50%

4. 7.4%

7. $16\frac{2}{3}\%$

2. 45%

5. 31%

8. 62.5%

3. $33\frac{1}{3}\%$

6. 125%

9. $21\frac{1}{4}\%$

Working with Percents

80% of 30 = ___
$\dfrac{80}{100} = \dfrac{x}{30}$
$100x = 2400$
$x = 24$

1. 20% of 110 = ____   3. 88% of 15 = ____

2. 25% of 45 = ____   4. $9\frac{1}{2}$% of 20 = ____

___% of 40 = 10
$\dfrac{x}{100} = \dfrac{10}{40}$
$40x = 1000$
$x = 25$ 25%

1. ____% of 25 = 15   3. ____% of 4 = 7

2. ____% of 30 = 10   4. ____% of 75 = 33

II.

50% of ___ = 65
$\dfrac{50}{100} = \dfrac{65}{x}$
$50x = 6500$
$x = 130$

1. 20% of ____ = 15   3. 25% of ____ = 19

2. 80% of ____ = 56   4. $33\frac{1}{3}$% of ___ = 41

       0-88012-866-6

Problems with Percents

1. In a group of 60 children, twelve have brown eyes. What percent have brown eyes?

2. A salesman makes a 5% commission on all he sells. How much does he have to sell to make $1500?

3. A sales tax of $5\frac{3}{4}$% is charged on a blouse priced at $42. How much sales tax must be paid?

4. A baby weighed 7.6 pounds at birth and $9\frac{1}{2}$ pounds after 6 weeks. What was the percent increase?

5. A scale model of a building is 8% of actual size. If the model is 1.2 meters tall, how tall is the building?

 0-88012-866-6

Can You De-Code This Puzzle?

Decipher the code and perform the indicated operations.

.3	$\frac{1}{20}$	2.1
$3\frac{1}{10}$	2.8	$\frac{8}{25}$
4	.1	$\frac{1}{2}$

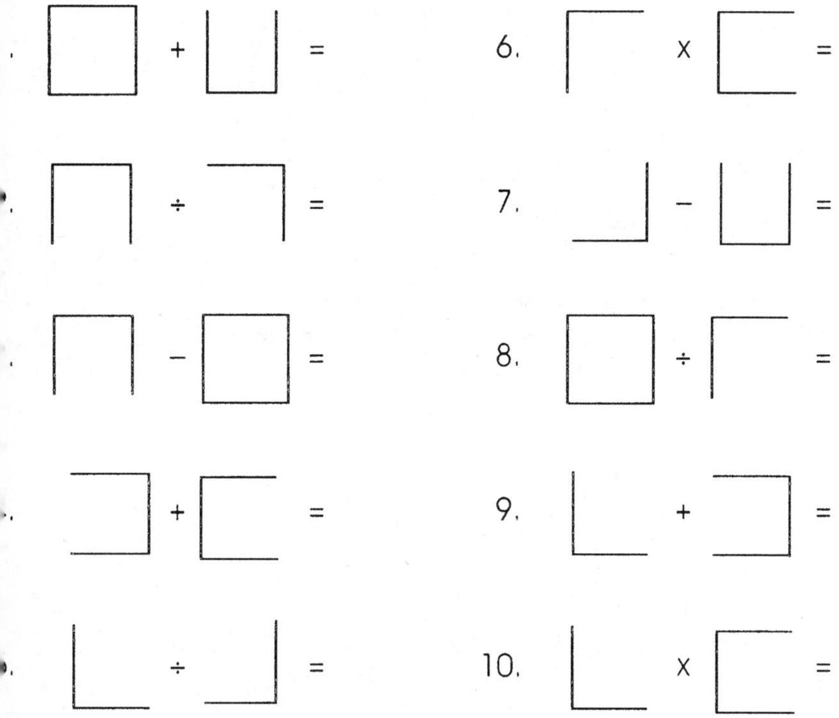

1. ☐ + ⊔ =

6. ⌐ x ☐ =

2. �⌐ ÷ ⌐ =

7. ⌐ − ⊔ =

3. ⌐ − ☐ =

8. ☐ ÷ ⌐ =

4. ⌐ + ☐ =

9. ⌐ + ⌐ =

5. ⌐ ÷ ⌐ =

10. ⌐ x ☐ =

Integers

Keep in mind...
**To suceed — Do the best you can, where you are,
with what you have.**

Positive and Negative Numbers

 = +6

1.

2.

3.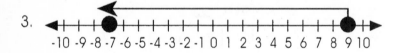

4.

5.

26 0-88012-866-6

Adding Integers (Number Line)

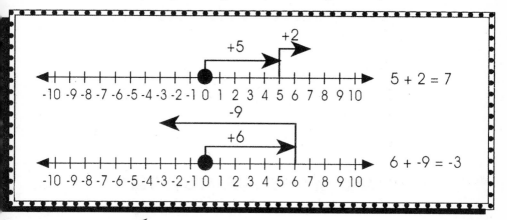

$5 + 2 = 7$

$6 + -9 = -3$

1.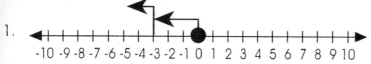

2.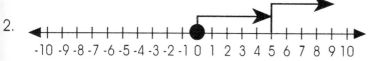

3.

4.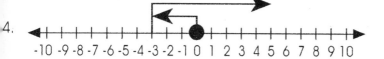

5.

6.

0-88012-866-6

Adding Integers with Like Signs

$$5 + 5 \quad = \quad 10$$

2 positives   positive

$$-3 + -12 \quad = \quad -15$$

2 negatives   negative

1. 6 + 8

2. -9 + -23

3. 25 + 37

4. -85 + -19

5. 132 + 899

6. -104 + -597

7. 19 + 42 + 647

8. -29 + -108 + -337 + -503

      0-88012-866-6

Adding Integers with Unlike Signs

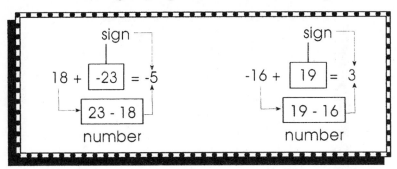

1. 2 + -8

2. -19 + 8

3. 25 + -5

4. -16 + 32

5. -319 + 319

6. -285 + 116

7. 46 + -29

8. -8 + 8

9. 852 + -468

10. -98 + 104

11. -63 + 41

12. 418 + -586

0-88012-866-6

Subtracting Integers

$$6 - 11 = 6 + \text{-}11 = \text{-}5$$
add the opposite

$$26 - \text{-}67 = 26 + 67 = 93$$
add the opposite

1. $19 - 23$

2. $\text{-}8 - 7$

3. $35 - 20$

4. $\text{-}46 - \text{-}18$

5. $\text{-}118 - 12$

6. $7 - \text{-}103$

7. $211 - 108$

8. $\text{-}9 - \text{-}16$

9. $63 - 72$

10. $\text{-}93 - 117$

11. $45 - \text{-}50$

12. $\text{-}18 - \text{-}12$

Adding & Subtracting Integers

1. -6 + -8

2. -10 – 3

3. -14 + 20

4. 31 – -9

5. -17 + 9

6. -8 – -27

7. -33 – 36

8. 19 + -32

9. 112 – -52

10. 0 – -7

11. 24 + -24

12. 508 – 678

13. -23 – -28

14. 0 – 31

15. -40 – 35

16. 73 + -19

17. -231 – -231

18. -107 + -293

19. 52 + -41 – 60

20. -85 – -106 + 18

Multiplying Integers

$$(4)(4) = 16 \qquad (-8)(-6) = 48 \qquad (-5)(10) = -50$$

+ • + = +   - • - = +   - • + = -

Like Signs ⟹ Positive   Unlike ⟹ Negative
                                    Signs

1. (-3) (-6)

2. (14) (-4)

3. (25) (2)

4. (20) (-49)

5. (75) (15)

6. (-30) (-30)

7. (-17) (23)

8. (-218) (-32)

9. (31) (-31) (31)

10. (-4) (-18) (28)

11. (-53) (-14) (-7)

12. (32) (125) (11)

Dividing Integers

$$\frac{-24}{-8} = 3 \qquad\qquad -32 \div 4 = -8$$

$$\frac{-}{-} = + \qquad\qquad - \div + = -$$

Like Signs ⟹ Positive   Unlike Signs ⟹ Negative

1. $-49 \div 7$

2. $100 \div -4$

3. $-75 \div -15$

4. $-84 \div 21$

5. $-120 \div 5$

6. $57 \div -19$

7. $\dfrac{17}{-17}$

8. $\dfrac{-72}{-18}$

9. $\dfrac{-195}{13}$

10. $\dfrac{-23}{-1}$

11. $\dfrac{200}{10}$

12. $\dfrac{270}{-45}$

 0-88012-866-6

Mixed Practice with Integers

1. -41 + -125

2. 79 − 88

3. -3 • -4

4. $\dfrac{125}{-5}$

5. 19 • -24

6. $\dfrac{-123}{41}$

7. 82 + -95

8. 27 − -46

9. -31 − -32

10. $\dfrac{-825}{-33}$

11. -34 + 52 + -18

12. 14 • -12 • 3

13. $\dfrac{-185}{5}$ • -4

14. 76 − 19 + -60

15. 17 − -12 - 22

16. 100 • -4 • 40

17. $\dfrac{54}{-9} + \dfrac{33}{11} + \dfrac{24}{8}$

18. -51 ÷ 17

19. 4 − 8 + -9

20. $\dfrac{-98}{49}$ • -10

34   0-88012-866-6

Problems with Integers

1. An elevator started at the first floor and went up 18 floors. It then came down 11 floors and went back up 16. At what floor was it stopped?

2. At midnight, the temperature was 30° F. By 6:00 a.m., it had dropped 5° and by noon, it it had increased by 11°. What was the temperature at noon?

3. Some number added to 5 is equal to -11. Find the number.

4. From the top of a mountain to the floor of the valley below is 4392 feet. If the valley is 93 feet below sea level, what is the height of the mountain?

0-88012-866-6

 Keep in mind...
Luck may sometimes help but work always does.

Adding and Subtracting Rational Numbers

$$-3 + -2 + 2\frac{1}{2} = -5 + 2\frac{1}{2} = -4\frac{2}{2} + 2\frac{1}{2} = -2\frac{1}{2}$$

1. $-1.6 + 1\frac{7}{10}$

   (Hint: $1\frac{7}{10} = 1.7$)

5. $\frac{1}{2} + 1\frac{1}{2} - 1\frac{1}{3}$

6. $6.75 - 3\frac{1}{2} + 2.55$

   (Hint: $3\frac{5}{10} = 3.5$)

2. $0 - 6\frac{1}{2} + -3$

3. $-\frac{3}{4} + 5 - \frac{1}{2}$

7. $3\frac{3}{7} - -1\frac{1}{7} + \frac{3}{7}$

4. $9 - 10.2 + -8.6$

8. $-7 - -2\frac{3}{4} + -5\frac{1}{4}$

0-88012-866-6

Keep in mind...
If you put forth 1/2 the effort, you only get a fraction of the results.

Simplifying Fractions

Numerator Smaller than Denominator

$$\frac{4}{8} \div \frac{4}{4} \text{ (greatest common denominator)} = \frac{1}{2}$$

1. $\frac{6}{9}$ — $\frac{2}{3}$
2. $\frac{10}{25}$ — $\frac{2}{5}$
3. $\frac{7}{14}$ — $\frac{1}{2}$
4. $\frac{8}{24}$ — $\frac{1}{3}$
5. $\frac{36}{60}$ — $\frac{3}{5}$
6. $\frac{18}{36}$ — $\frac{1}{2}$
7. $\frac{8}{28}$ — $\frac{2}{7}$
8. $\frac{21}{45}$ — $\frac{7}{15}$
9. $\frac{12}{40}$ — $\frac{3}{10}$
10. $\frac{19}{57}$ — $\frac{1}{3}$
11. $\frac{20}{28}$ — $5/7$
12. $\frac{18}{44}$ — $9/22$

...More Simplifying

Numerator larger than denominator

$$\frac{17}{4} = 4\frac{1}{4}$$
Improper fraction

$$\frac{12}{7} = \frac{7}{7} + \frac{5}{7} = 1 + \frac{5}{7} = 1\frac{5}{7}$$
Mixed Numeral

Write answers as improper fractions.

1. $\frac{15}{6}$ — $\frac{5}{2}$ $2\frac{1}{2}$
2. $\frac{36}{27}$ — $\frac{4}{3}$ $1\frac{1}{3}$
3. $\frac{40}{14}$ — $\frac{20}{7}$ $2\frac{6}{7}$
4. $\frac{20}{12}$ — $\frac{5}{3}$ $1\frac{2}{3}$

5. $\frac{52}{7}$ — $\frac{52}{7}$ $1\frac{4}{7}$
6. $\frac{33}{24}$ — $\frac{11}{8}$ $1\frac{3}{8}$
7. $\frac{28}{24}$ — $\frac{7}{6}$ $1\frac{1}{6}$
8. $\frac{66}{33}$ — $\frac{22}{9}$ $2\frac{4}{9}$

Now go back and write the answers as mixed numerals.

Adding and Subtracting Fractions

I. Like Denominators

$$\frac{1}{8} + \frac{3}{8} = \frac{4}{8} = \frac{1}{2}$$

1. $\frac{2}{9} + \frac{5}{9}$ — $\frac{7}{9}$
2. $\frac{3}{4} - \frac{1}{4}$ — $\frac{1}{2}$
3. $\frac{9}{18} + \frac{5}{18}$ — $\frac{14}{15}$
4. $\frac{19}{20} - \frac{14}{20}$ — $\frac{1}{4}$
5. $\frac{27}{38} + \frac{14}{38}$ — $1\frac{1}{19}$
6. $\frac{38}{60} - \frac{17}{60}$ — $\frac{3}{10}$

7. $\frac{17}{20} + \frac{23}{20}$ — 2
8. $\frac{25}{13} - \frac{12}{13}$ — 1
9. $\frac{11}{18} + \frac{16}{18}$ — $1\frac{1}{2}$
10. $\frac{17}{48} - \frac{14}{48}$ — $\frac{1}{16}$
11. $\frac{7}{45} + \frac{8}{45}$ — $\frac{1}{3}$
12. $\frac{33}{50} - \frac{17}{50}$ — $8/25$

...More Adding and Subtracting

II. Unlike Denominators

$$\frac{7}{9} + \frac{1}{4} = \frac{28}{36} + \frac{9}{36} = \frac{37}{36}$$
36 is the least common multiple

1. $\frac{2}{3} + \frac{5}{9}$ — $1\frac{2}{9}$
2. $\frac{4}{5} - \frac{3}{4}$ — $\frac{1}{20}$
3. $\frac{5}{6} + \frac{7}{12}$ — $1\frac{5}{12}$
4. $\frac{11}{12} - \frac{2}{3}$ — $\frac{1}{3}$
5. $\frac{11}{12} + \frac{5}{8}$ — $1\frac{13}{24}$
6. $\frac{1}{2} - \frac{4}{9}$ — $\frac{1}{18}$

7. $\frac{13}{36} + \frac{5}{12}$ — $\frac{7}{9}$
8. $\frac{7}{8} - \frac{3}{10}$ — $\frac{23}{40}$
9. $\frac{4}{9} + \frac{13}{15}$ — $1\frac{14}{45}$
10. $\frac{5}{12} + \frac{5}{18}$ — $\frac{5}{36}$
11. $\frac{5}{8} + \frac{3}{9}$ — $\frac{67}{72}$
12. $\frac{5}{12} - \frac{3}{15}$ — $\frac{13}{60}$

...And More Adding and Subtracting

III. Mixed Numerals

$$3\frac{1}{8} + 5\frac{1}{4} = 3\frac{11}{24} + 6\frac{21}{24} + 8\frac{22}{24} = 9\frac{22}{24} = 9\frac{1}{3}$$

1. $1\frac{1}{2} + 2\frac{1}{4}$ — $3\frac{3}{4}$
2. $5\frac{7}{10} - 1\frac{1}{6}$ — $4\frac{8}{15}$
3. $8\frac{3}{8} + 9\frac{2}{3}$ — $18\frac{1}{24}$
4. $6 - 2\frac{3}{11}$ — $3\frac{8}{11}$
5. $2\frac{1}{16} + 2\frac{1}{4}$ — $4\frac{13}{16}$
6. $7\frac{7}{8} - 7\frac{5}{12}$ — $\frac{11}{24}$

7. $4\frac{1}{2} + 6\frac{3}{5}$ — $10\frac{9}{10}$
8. $5\frac{1}{2} - \frac{11}{15}$ — $4\frac{23}{30}$
9. $1\frac{3}{8} + 4$ — $5\frac{3}{8}$
10. $6\frac{7}{8} - 6\frac{1}{8}$ — $\frac{5}{8}$
11. $7\frac{1}{8} + 1\frac{1}{2} + 2\frac{5}{9}$ — $11\frac{31}{36}$
12. $8\frac{1}{8} - 7\frac{3}{12}$ — $\frac{5}{12}$

Multiplying Fractions

Rewrite

$$2\frac{1}{2} \cdot 1\frac{3}{8} = \frac{9}{2} \cdot \frac{6}{5} = \frac{3}{2} \cdot \frac{9}{3} \cdot \frac{18}{5} = 3\frac{3}{5}$$

Rewrite

1. $\frac{1}{2} \cdot \frac{5}{6}$ — $\frac{5}{12}$
2. $3 \cdot \frac{1}{2}$ — $1\frac{1}{2}$
3. $\frac{2}{3} \cdot \frac{1}{5}$ — $\frac{2}{15}$
4. $\frac{16}{27} \cdot \frac{25}{16}$ — $2\frac{26}{27}$
5. $\frac{8}{21} \cdot 2\frac{7}{16}$ — $\frac{13}{14}$
6. $1\frac{2}{7} \cdot 2\frac{1}{4}$ — $3\frac{4}{7}$

7. $5\frac{7}{8} \cdot 4$ — $23\frac{1}{2}$
8. $\frac{5}{7} \cdot \frac{7}{5}$ — 1
9. $3\frac{2}{3} \cdot \frac{17}{22}$ — $2\frac{5}{6}$
10. $\frac{1}{2} \cdot \frac{6}{11} \cdot \frac{1}{2}$ — $\frac{9}{55}$
11. $9\frac{1}{3} \cdot 1\frac{5}{7} \cdot \frac{3}{4}$ — 12
12. $2\frac{1}{4} \cdot 6 \cdot 1\frac{1}{9}$ — 15

Dividing Fractions

Invert and Multiply

$$1\frac{1}{2} \div 3\frac{3}{7} = \frac{3}{2} \div \frac{24}{7} = \frac{3}{2} \cdot \frac{7}{24} = \frac{7}{16}$$
Rewrite

1. $\frac{3}{5} \div \frac{1}{2}$ — $\frac{6}{5}$
2. $\frac{17}{9} \div \frac{8}{9}$ — $2\frac{1}{8}$
3. $6\frac{2}{3} \div 5$ — $1\frac{1}{3}$
4. $1\frac{7}{9} \div 4\frac{2}{9}$ — $\frac{8}{19}$
5. $\frac{15}{14} \div \frac{5}{14}$ — $10\frac{1}{2}$
6. $\frac{11}{12} \div \frac{13}{12}$ — $\frac{22}{39}$

7. $4 \div 4\frac{2}{5}$ — $\frac{10}{11}$
8. $3\frac{1}{4} \div 4\frac{3}{8}$ — $\frac{26}{35}$
9. $\frac{6}{15} \div \frac{9}{10}$ — $\frac{4}{9}$
10. $\frac{7}{9} \div 2\frac{1}{3}$ — $\frac{3}{9}$
11. $9\frac{3}{8} \div 3\frac{3}{4}$ — $2\frac{1}{2}$
12. $5\frac{1}{4} \div \frac{21}{4}$ — 1

Mixed Practice with Fractions

1. $1\frac{1}{3} \cdot \frac{8}{9} \cdot 2\frac{1}{8}$ — $2\frac{1}{6}$
2. $\frac{4}{7} \div \frac{11}{16}$ — $\frac{44}{28}$
3. $5 \cdot 6\frac{1}{4}$ — $\frac{4}{5}$
4. $\frac{11}{17} \div \frac{15}{17}$ — $1\frac{4}{7}$
5. $7\frac{2}{5} - 2\frac{1}{4}$ — $5\frac{3}{20}$
6. $2\frac{2}{3} \cdot 3\frac{1}{2}$ — $9\frac{3}{5}$
7. $2\frac{4}{7} \cdot \frac{20}{21}$ — $2\frac{6}{10}$
8. $\frac{42}{11} \div \frac{7}{2}$ — $\frac{12}{22}$
9. $\frac{5}{12} \cdot \frac{7}{24} \cdot \frac{31}{32}$ — $\frac{281}{312}$
10. $\frac{13}{25} \cdot \frac{10}{39} \cdot \frac{18}{5}$ — 1

11. $6\frac{1}{4} - 3\frac{2}{3}$ — $2\frac{7}{12}$
12. $\frac{7}{9} \cdot \frac{8}{3}$ — $2\frac{1}{10}$
13. $8\frac{1}{3} + 2\frac{3}{10}$ — $10\frac{19}{30}$
14. $11\frac{1}{2} - \frac{5}{9}$ — $10\frac{11}{18}$
15. $\frac{2}{13} \cdot \frac{3}{7} \cdot 4\frac{1}{2}$ — $2\frac{4}{7}$
16. $5\frac{3}{4} \cdot 1\frac{2}{15}$ — 5
17. $4\frac{1}{8} \cdot 2\frac{6}{10} - 6\frac{1}{2}$ — 0
18. $(1\frac{5}{9} \cdot 3) \cdot \frac{1}{3}$ — 14
19. $1\frac{4}{5} \cdot 1\frac{1}{5} \cdot 1\frac{1}{30}$ — 4
20. $\frac{7}{9} \cdot (\frac{11}{12} \cdot \frac{33}{7})$ — 1

Problems with Fractions

1. If $1\frac{1}{2}$ pounds of bananas sell for 80¢ and $1\frac{1}{3}$ pounds of apples sell for 90¢, which fruit is cheaper?

   The bananas are cheaper.
   64¢/lb

2. A cake recipe calls for $\frac{3}{4}$ teaspoon salt, $1\frac{1}{3}$ teaspoons baking powder, 1 teaspoon baking soda and $\frac{2}{3}$ teaspoon cinnamon. How many total teaspoons of dry ingredients are used?

   $3\frac{3}{4}$ teaspoons

3. A baseball team played 35 games and won $\frac{4}{7}$ of them. How many games were won? **20**
   How many games were lost? **15**

4. During 4 days, the price of the stock of PEV Corporation went up $\frac{1}{2}$ of a point, down $\frac{1}{3}$ of a point, down $\frac{3}{5}$ of a point and up $\frac{4}{15}$ of a point. What was the net change?

   down $\frac{2}{15}$

Changing Fractions to Decimals

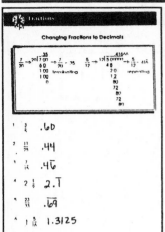

1. $\frac{3}{5}$ .60

2. $\frac{11}{25}$ .44

3. $\frac{7}{15}$ .4\overline{6}

4. $2\frac{1}{3}$ 2.\overline{3}

5. $\frac{23}{33}$.\overline{69}

6. $1\frac{5}{16}$ 1.3125

Keep in mind...
Don't wait for things to be just right before you get started. Start now!

Rounding Decimals

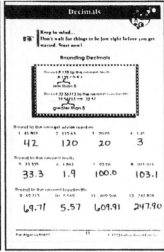

Round to the nearest whole number
1.   42   2.   120   3.   20   4.   3

Round to the nearest tenth
5.   33.3   6.   1.9   7.   100.0   8.   103.1

Round to the nearest hundredth
9.   69.71   10.   5.57   11.   609.91   12.   247.90

Multiplying and Dividing by 10, 100, etc.

1.   481   7.   439.500

2.   3.768   8.   .000075

3.   460   9.   22.74

4.   .000712   10.   900

5.   54   11.   .618

6.   27.5   12.   .039006

Adding and Subtracting Decimals

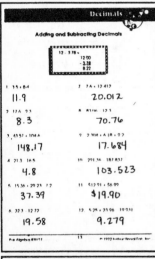

1.   11.9   7.   20.012

2.   8.3   8.   70.76

3.   148.17   9.   17.684

4.   4.8   10.   103.523

5.   37.39   11. $19.90

6.   19.58   12.   9.279

Multiplying Decimals

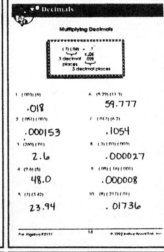

1.   .018   6.   59.777

2.   .000153   7.   .1054

3.   2.6   8.   .000027

4.   48.0   9.   .000008

5.   23.94   10.   .01736

Dividing Decimals

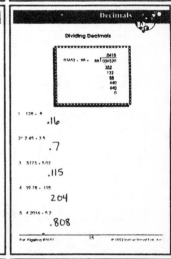

1.   .16

2.   .7

3.   .115

4.   204

5.   .808

Mixed Practice with Decimals

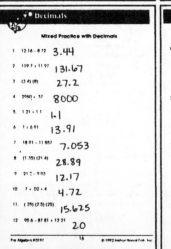

1.   3.44

2.   131.67

3.   27.2

4.   8000

5.   1.1

6.   13.91

7.   7.053

8.   28.89

9.   12.17

10.   4.72

11.   15.625

12.   20

Problems with Decimals

1. Jim's gas credit card bill was $80.97 for June, $41.35 for July and $65.08 for August. What were his total charges for the summer?

$187.40

2. One cup of hot chocolate can be made with 18 ounces of hot chocolate mix. How many cups can be made from a 648 ounce canister of mix?

36 cups

3. Karl's car payments are $215.37 per month for the next three years. What will be the total amount he will pay for his car?

$7753.32

4. The dress Sally wants costs $85.15. If the price was reduced by $12.78, how much will she pay?

$72.37

More Changing Fractions to Decimals

1. $\frac{3}{8}$ .375   6. $5\frac{1}{8}$ 5.125

2. $\frac{8}{15}$ .5\overline{3}   7. $1\frac{4}{5}$ 1.8

3. $\frac{27}{32}$ .84375   8. $\frac{10}{35}$.\overline{285714}

4. $\frac{23}{30}$ .7\overline{6}   9. $\frac{9}{15}$ .6

5. $\frac{4}{7}$.\overline{571428}   10. $2\frac{3}{8}$ 2.375

Decimals

Dividing Decimals

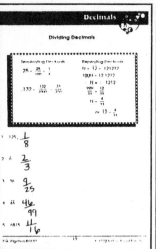

Repeating Decimals / Terminating Decimals

$1. \ 1.25, \ \dfrac{1}{8}$

$2. \ \dfrac{2}{3}$

$3. \ \dfrac{9}{25}$

$4. \ \dfrac{46}{99}$

$5. \ \dfrac{11}{6}$

Ratios, Proportions and Percents

Keep in mind
Life is 10% what you make it
and 90% how you take it.

Ratios and Proportions

I. Write each ratio as a fraction in simplest form.

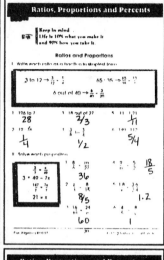

$3 \text{ to } 12 \rightarrow \dfrac{3}{12} = \dfrac{1}{4}$ $65 : 35 \rightarrow \dfrac{65}{35} = \dfrac{13}{7}$

$6 \text{ out of } 40 \rightarrow \dfrac{6}{40} = \dfrac{3}{20}$

$1. \ \dfrac{1}{28}$ $4. \ \dfrac{2}{3}$ $5. \ \dfrac{4}{7}$

$2. \ \dfrac{1}{4}$ $3. \ \dfrac{1}{2}$ $6. \ \dfrac{5}{4}$

II. Solve each proportion.

36 $\dfrac{18}{5}$

$\dfrac{8}{5}$ 1.2

60 1

Ratios, Proportions and Percents

Problems Using Proportions

Three loaves of bread cost $3.87.
How much do 2 loaves cost?

$\dfrac{\text{number of loaves}}{\text{cost}} = \dfrac{3}{3.87} = \dfrac{2}{x}$

$3x = 2 \cdot 3.87$

$\dfrac{3x}{3} = \dfrac{7.74}{3}$

$x = 2.58$

2 loaves cost $2.58

1. **25 pounds**

2. **5.6 hours**

3. **13.5 ounces**

4. **13 hours**

Ratios, Proportions and Percents

Percents

Write each expression as a percent.

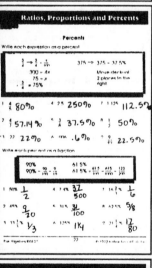

$\dfrac{3}{4} \rightarrow \dfrac{3}{4} = \dfrac{x}{100}$ $.375 \rightarrow .375 = 37.5\%$

$300 = 4x$ Move decimal

$75 = x$ 2 places to the right

$\dfrac{3}{4} = 75\%$

$1. \ 80\%$ $4. \ 250\%$ $7. \ 112.5\%$

$2. \ 57.14\%$ $5. \ 37.5\%$ $8. \ 50\%$

$3. \ 22\%$ $6. \ .6\%$ $9. \ 22.5\%$

Write each percent as a fraction.

$90\% \rightarrow \dfrac{90}{100} = \dfrac{9}{10}$ $61.5\% \rightarrow \dfrac{61.5}{100} = \dfrac{615}{1000} = \dfrac{123}{200}$

$1. \ \dfrac{1}{2}$ $4. \ \dfrac{37}{500}$ $7. \ \dfrac{1}{6}$

$2. \ \dfrac{9}{10}$ $5. \ \dfrac{31}{100}$ $8. \ \dfrac{5}{8}$

$3. \ \dfrac{1}{3}$ $6. \ 1\dfrac{1}{4}$ $9. \ \dfrac{17}{80}$

Ratios, Proportions and Percents

Working with Percents

I.

80% of 30 $1. \ 20\% \text{ of } 110 = 22$ $3. \ 88\% \text{ of } 15 = 13.2$

$\dfrac{80}{100} = \dfrac{x}{30}$

$100x = 2400$ $2. \ 25\% \text{ of } 45 = 11.25$ $4. \ 9\dfrac{1}{2}\% \text{ of } 20 = 1.9$

$x = 24$

II.

% of 40 = 10 $1. \ 60 \text{ of } 25 = 15$ $3. \ 75 \text{ of } 4 = 7$

$\dfrac{x}{100} = \dfrac{10}{40}$

$40x = 1000$ $2. \ 33\dfrac{1}{3}\% \text{ of } x = 10$ $4. \ 44 \text{ of } 15 = 11$

$x = 25$ 25%

III.

80% of = 45 $1. \ 20\% \text{ of } 75 = 15$ $3. \ 25\% \text{ of } 76 = 19$

$\dfrac{80}{100} = \dfrac{45}{x}$

$50x = 6500$ $2. \ 80\% \text{ of } 70 = 56$ $4. \ 11\dfrac{1}{2}\% \text{ of } = 123$

$x = 130$

Ratios, Proportions and Percents

Problems with Percents

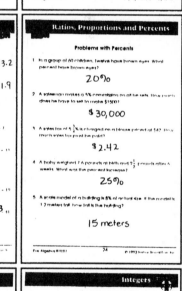

1. In a group of 60 children, twelve have brown eyes. What percent have brown eyes?

20%

2. A salesman makes a 6% commission on all he sells. How much does he have to sell to make $1500?

$30,000

3. A sales tax of 5$\frac{3}{4}$% is charged on a blouse priced at $42. How much sales tax must be paid?

$2.42

4. A baby weighed 7.6 pounds at birth and 9$\frac{1}{2}$ pounds after 6 weeks. What was the percent increase?

25%

5. A scale model of a building is 8% of actual size. If the model is 1.2 meters tall, how tall is the building?

15 meters

Ratios, Proportions and Percents

Can You De-Code This Puzzle?

Decipher the code and perform the indicated operations.

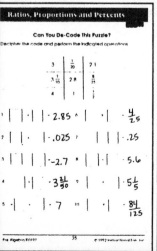

$1. \ -2.85$ $\dfrac{4}{25}$

$2. \ .025$ $.25$

$3. \ -2.7$ 5.6

$4. \ -3\dfrac{21}{50}$ $5\dfrac{1}{5}$

$5. \ 7$ $-\dfrac{84}{125}$

Integers

Keep in mind
To succeed — Do the best you can, where you are,
with what you have.

Positive and Negative Numbers

$= +6$

$1. \ +3$

$2. \ -2$

$3. \ -16$

$4. \ +5$

$5. \ -4$

Integers

Adding Integers (Number Line)

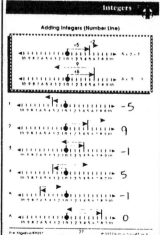

$5 + 2 = 7$

$4 + 2 = 6$

$1. \ -5$

$2. \ 9$

$3. \ -1$

$4. \ 5$

$5. \ -1$

$6. \ 0$

Adding Integers with Like Signs

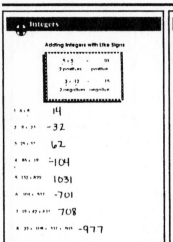

1. 14
2. −32
3. 62
4. −104
5. 1031
6. −701
7. 708
8. −977

Adding Integers with Unlike Signs

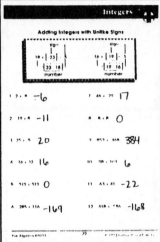

1. −6
2. −11
3. 20
4. 16
5. 0
6. −169
7. 17
8. 0
9. 384
10. 6
11. −22
12. −168

Subtracting Integers

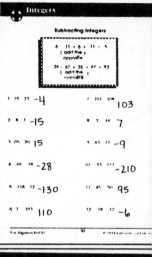

1. −4
2. −15
3. 15
4. −28
5. −130
6. 110
7. 103
8. 7
9. −9
10. −210
11. 95
12. −6

Adding & Subtracting Integers

1. −14
2. −13
3. 6
4. 40
5. −8
6. 19
7. −69
8. −13
9. 164
10. −7
11. 0
12. −170
13. 5
14. −31
15. −75
16. 54
17. 0
18. −400
19. −49
20. 39

Multiplying Integers

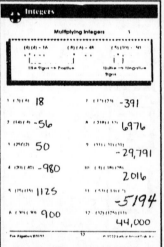

1. 18
2. −56
3. 50
4. −980
5. 1125
6. 900
7. −391
8. 6976
9. −29,791
10. 2016
11. −5194
12. 44,000

Dividing Integers

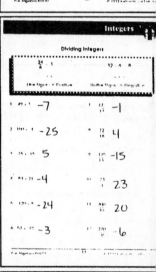

1. −7
2. −25
3. 5
4. −4
5. −24
6. −3
7. −1
8. 4
9. −15
10. 23
11. 20
12. −6

Mixed Practice with Integers

1. −166
2. −9
3. 12
4. −25
5. −456
6. −3
7. −13
8. 73
9. 1
10. 25
11. 0
12. −504
13. 148
14. −3
15. 7
16. −16,000
17. 0
18. −3
19. −13
20. 20

Problems with Integers

1. 23

2. 36°

3. −16

4. 4299 feet

Adding and Subtracting Rational Numbers

1. .1
2. −9½
3. 3¾
4. −9.8
5. 2/3
6. 5.8
7. 5
8. −9½

Rational Numbers

Multiplying and Dividing Rational Numbers

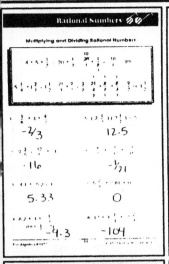

$-\frac{2}{3}$ 12.5

-16 $-\frac{1}{21}$

5.33 0

-4.3 -104

Rational Numbers

Order of Operations with Rational Numbers

1. $-1\frac{2}{3}$
2. -10
3. -6
4. 19
5. 5
6. -74
7. 3

Rational Numbers

Comparing Rational Numbers

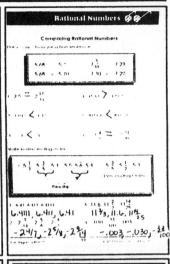

$6.411,\ 6.411,\ 6.41$ $11\frac{2}{3},\ 11.6,\ 11\frac{4}{25}$

$-2\frac{4}{7},\ -2\frac{5}{8},\ -2\frac{14}{}$ $-.003,\ -.030,\ -\frac{22}{100}$

Rational Numbers

The Flip Quiz

1. 50705.345 She solos
2. 53045.514 his shoes
3. 53704 holes
4. 31908 BUGIE
5. 0.04008 BOO HOO

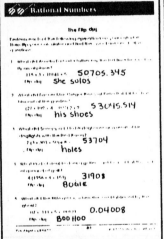

Equations

Open Sentences

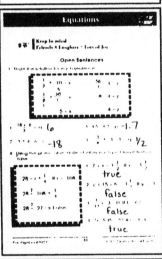

-6 -1.7

-18 $\frac{1}{2}$

true
false
false
true

Equations

Evaluating Expressions

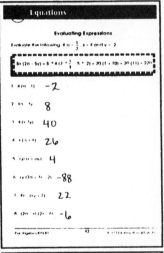

1. -2
2. 8
3. 40
4. 26
5. 4
6. -88
7. 22
8. -6

Equations

Simplifying Expressions

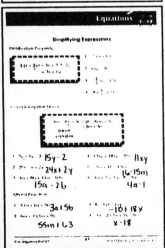

$15y-2$ $11xy$
$24x+2y$ $16-15m$
$15a-2b$ $4a-1$

$3a+5b$ $-10+18x$
$55m+63$ $x-18$

Equations

Solving Addition Equations

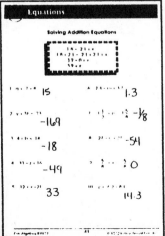

1. 15 1.3
2. -169 $-\frac{1}{8}$
3. -18 -54
4. -49 0
5. 33 14.3

Equations

Solving Subtraction Equations

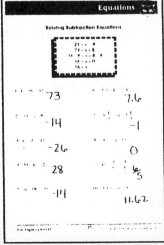

73 7.6
-14 -1
-26 0
28 $\frac{6}{5}$
-11 11.62

E

0-88012-866-6

Solving Multiplication Equations

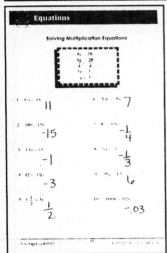

11   7

-15 $-\frac{1}{4}$

-1 $-\frac{1}{3}$

-3   6

$\frac{1}{2}$ -.03

Solving Division Equations

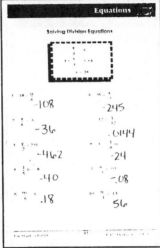

-108   -245

-36   .6144

-462   -24

-40   -.08

.18   56

Mixed Practice with Equations

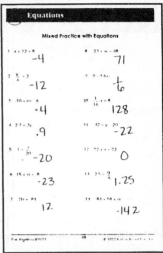

-4   71

-12   6

-4   128

.9   -22

-20   0

-23   1.25

12   -142

Solving Equations with 2 Operations

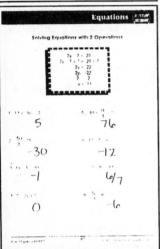

5   76

-30   -12

-1   6/7

0   -6

Solving Equations with Negative Variables

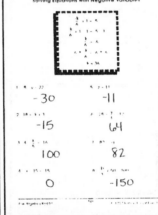

-30   -11

-15   64

100   82

0   -150

Solving Equations Using the Distributive Property

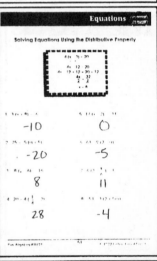

-10   0

-20   -5

8   11

28   -4

Solving Equations — Variables on Both Sides

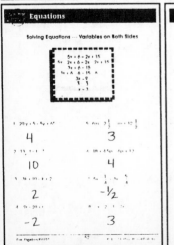

4   3

10   4

2   -1/2

-2   3

Writing Algebraic Expressions

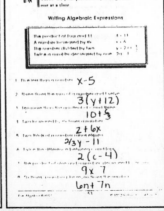

1. $x-5$

2. $3(y+12)$

3. $10+\frac{n}{3}$

4. $2+6x$

5. $\frac{2}{3}y-11$

6. $2(c-4)$

7. $9x$

8. $6n+7n$

Solving Problems

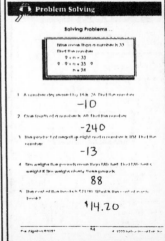

1. -10

2. -240

3. -13

4. 88

5. $14.20

More Problems

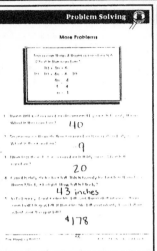

1. **40**
2. **-9**
3. **20**
4. **43 inches**
5. **$178**

And More Problems

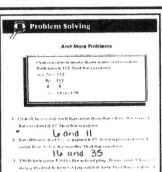

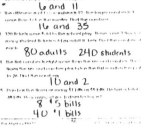

1. **6 and 11**
2. **16 and 35**
3. **80 adults   240 students**
4. **10 and 2**
5. **8 $5 bills   40 $1 bills**

And Still More Problems

1. **6**
2. **-4**
3. **width -18 feet   length - 40 feet**
4. **Mike is 15.**
5. **49 inches**

Keep in mind...
You only fail when you stop trying

Number Lines

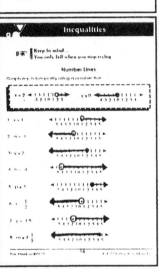

Solving Inequalities with Addition or Subtraction

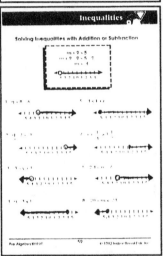

Solving Inequalities with Multiplication or Division

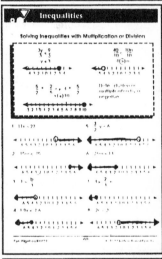

Solving Inequalities with More Than One Operation

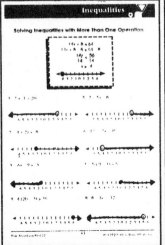

Solving Inequalities with Variables on Both Sides

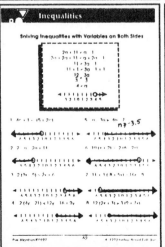

Mixed Practice with Inequalities

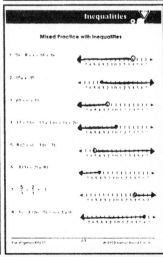

Inequalities

A Logical Conclusion

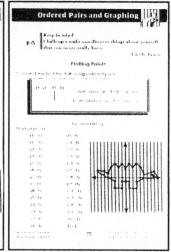

Ordered Pairs and Graphing

Keep in mind

Plotting Points

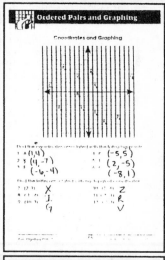

Ordered Pairs and Graphing

Coordinates and Graphing

A $(1,4)$ $(-5,5)$
$(4,-7)$ $(2,-5)$
$(-6,-4)$ $(-8,1)$

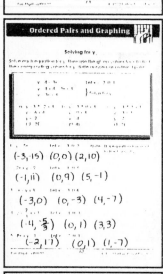

Ordered Pairs and Graphing

Solving for y

$(-3,-15)$ $(0,0)$ $(2,10)$

$(-1,11)$ $(0,9)$ $(5,-1)$

$(-3,0)$ $(0,-3)$ $(4,-7)$

$\left(-4,\dfrac{-5}{3}\right)$ $(0,1)$ $(3,3)$

$(-2,17)$ $(0,1)$ $(1,-7)$

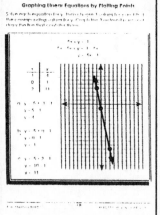

Ordered Pairs and Graphing

Graphing Linear Equations by Plotting Points

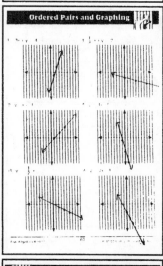

Ordered Pairs and Graphing

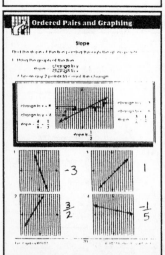

Slope

-3 1

$\dfrac{3}{2}$ $-\dfrac{1}{5}$

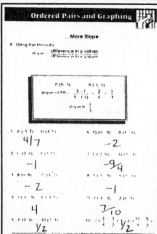

Ordered Pairs and Graphing

...More Slope

$$slope = \frac{\text{difference in } y \text{ values}}{\text{difference in } x \text{ values}}$$

$\dfrac{4}{7}$ -2

-1 $-\dfrac{9}{4}$

-2 -1

4 $\dfrac{7}{10}$

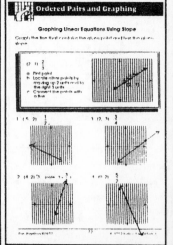

Ordered Pairs and Graphing

Graphing Linear Equations Using Slope

H

0-88012-866-6

Multiplying and Dividing Rational Numbers

$$-4 \cdot 5 \cdot \frac{1}{2} = -20 \cdot \frac{1}{2} = -\frac{\overset{10}{\cancel{20}}}{1} \cdot \frac{1}{\underset{1}{\cancel{2}}} = -\frac{10}{1} = -10$$

$$5\frac{1}{4} \cdot 1\frac{2}{7} \div 1\frac{1}{2} = \frac{21}{4} \cdot \frac{9}{7} \div \frac{3}{2} = \frac{\overset{3}{\cancel{21}}}{\underset{2}{\cancel{4}}} \cdot \frac{\overset{3}{\cancel{9}}}{\underset{1}{\cancel{7}}} \cdot \frac{\overset{1}{\cancel{2}}}{\underset{1}{\cancel{3}}} = \frac{9}{2} \text{ or } 4\frac{1}{2}$$

1. $-\dfrac{3}{8} \cdot 4 \cdot \dfrac{4}{9}$

2. $-9\dfrac{3}{5} \div \dfrac{12}{5} \cdot -4$

3. $-4.1 \cdot -5.2 \div 4$

4. $6.2 \cdot 3 \cdot -\dfrac{1}{2}$
   (Hint: $\frac{1}{2} = .5$)

5. $(-2\frac{1}{2})(-2\frac{1}{2}) \div .5$

6. $-\dfrac{6}{7} \cdot -\dfrac{5}{12} \cdot -\dfrac{2}{15}$

7. $5\dfrac{2}{3} \cdot 9.81 \cdot 0$

8. $12 \cdot 3\frac{1}{4} \cdot -2\frac{2}{3}$

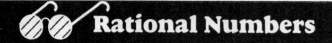

Order of Operations with Rational Numbers

$$-3 \bullet 5 + 2 = -15 + 2 = -13$$

$$2\frac{1}{2} \div (5+5) = \frac{5}{2} \div 10 = \frac{\cancel{5}^{1}}{2} \bullet \frac{1}{\cancel{10}_{2}} = \frac{1}{4}$$

1. $-28 \div 7 + 2\frac{1}{3}$

2. $\frac{1}{2}(-16 - 4)$

3. $-9 \div -3 + 4 \bullet -\frac{1}{4} - 20 \div 5$

4. $\frac{1}{3}[(-18 + 3) + (5 + 7) \div -4]$

5. $(8\frac{1}{3} + 3\frac{2}{3}) \div 4 - -16$

6. $\frac{(80 \bullet \frac{1}{2}) + 35}{-10 + 25}$

7. $2[-6(3 - 12) - 17]$

8. $\frac{1}{4}(20 + 72 \div -9)$

38 0-88012-866-6

Comparing Rational Numbers

Use <, > or = to make a true sentence.

$$5.68 \_\_\_ 5.7 \qquad\qquad -7\frac{3}{10} \_\_\_ -7.29$$
$$5.68 \ < \ 5.70 \qquad\qquad -7.30 \ < \ -7.29$$

1. $2.5 \_\_\_ 2\frac{17}{34}$

4. $15.62 \_\_\_ 1.562$

2. $1.049 \_\_\_ 1.49$

5. $8156.6 \_\_\_ 8166.6$

3. $-.\overline{3} \_\_\_ -.3$

6. $-7\frac{4}{5} \_\_\_ -7\frac{24}{30}$

Write in descending order.

$$5\frac{1}{2}, 5\frac{3}{5}, 5.4 \quad 5.5, 5.6, 5.4 \qquad 5\frac{3}{5}, 5\frac{1}{2}, 5.4$$

Rewrite

Descending Order

1. $6.41, 6.411, 6.4111$

3. $11.6, 11\frac{2}{3}, 11\frac{14}{25}$

2. $-2\frac{9}{14}, -2\frac{5}{8}, -2\frac{4}{7}$

4. $-.030, -\frac{33}{100}, -.003$

0-88012-866-6

The Flip dᴉɹⱢ

Perform each of the following operations on your calculator. Then flip your calculator and find the "word answer" to the questions.

1. What did Amelia Earhart's father say the first time he saw her fly an airplane?

    .115 x 3 + 10141 x 5 = _____

    Flip dᴉɹⱢ _____

2. What did Farmer MacGregor throw at Peter Rabbit to chase him out of the garden?

    (27 x 109 + 4 − .027) 2 x 9 = _____

    Flip dᴉɹⱢ _____

3. What did Snoopy add to his doghouse as a result of his dogfights with the Red Baron?

    7 (3 x 303 + 50) x 8 = _____

    Flip dᴉɹⱢ _____

4. What kind of double does a golfer want to avoid at the end of a round of golf?

    4 (1956 x 4 + 153) = _____

    Flip dᴉɹⱢ _____

5. What did the little girl say when she was frightened by the ghost?

    .07 x .111 x 5 + .00123 = _____

    Flip dᴉɹⱢ _____

👉 **Keep in mind...**
Friends × Laughter = Lots of Joy

Open Sentences

I. State the solution for each sentence.

$$\frac{1}{2} \cdot -10 = x$$

$$\frac{1}{\cancel{2}} \cdot \frac{\cancel{-10}^{-5}}{1} = x$$
$$1$$

$$-5 = x$$

$$\frac{-56}{-7} - 4 = z$$

$$8 - 4 = z$$

$$4 = z$$

1. $\dfrac{18 + -6}{2} = a$

2. $-3 \cdot 4 - 6 = c$

3. $4.5 - 6.2 = p$

4. $-\dfrac{3}{8} \cdot -4 - 1 = q$

II. Using the given value, state whether each problem is true or false.

$$28 = r \cdot \frac{1}{4}, \text{ if } r = -108$$

$$28 \overset{?}{=} -108 \cdot \frac{1}{4}$$

$$28 \overset{?}{=} -27 \Rightarrow \text{False}$$

1. $7 + x = 3\dfrac{1}{2}$, if $x = -3\dfrac{1}{2}$

2. $y + 15 \div 6 = -1\dfrac{1}{2}$, if $y = -3$

3. $\dfrac{f}{13} + -3 = 0$, if $f = 69$

4. $2x - 5.45 = .97$, if $x = 3.21$

41 0-88012-866-6

Evaluating Expressions

Evaluate the following, if $a = \dfrac{1}{2}$, $x = 4$ and $y = -2$.

$$5x\,(2a - 5y) = 5 \bullet 4\,\left(2 \bullet \dfrac{1}{2} - 5 \bullet -2\right) = 20\,(1 + 10) = 20\,(11) = 220$$

1. $4\,(a - 1)$

2. $4a - 3y$

3. $4\,(x\text{-}3y)$

4. $x\,(a + 6)$

5. $x\,(ax + ay)$

6. $xy\,(2a + 3x - 2)$

7. $4x - (xy + 2)$

8. $(2a - x)\,(2x - 6)$

---

42 0-88012-866-6

Simplifying Expressions

Distributive Property

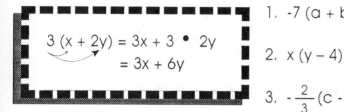

$3(x + 2y) = 3x + 3 \cdot 2y$
$= 3x + 6y$

1. $-7(a + b)$

2. $x(y - 4)$

3. $-\dfrac{2}{3}(c - 12)$

4. $-8\left(\dfrac{1}{2} + 6\right)$

Combining Like Terms

$6m - 4m + 3p = (6 - 4)m + 3p$
$= 2m + 3p$
same
variable

1. $9y + 6y - 2$

2. $25x - x + 2y$

3. $4a + 8b + 11a - 10b$

4. $13xy + 18xy - 20xy$

5. $-2m + 16 - 13m$

6. $4a + 7 + 3a - 8 - 3a$

Mixed Practice

1. $3(a + b) + 2b$

2. $6m + 7(7m + 9)$

3. $8 - 3(6 - 6x)$

4. $-6x - 2(-5x + 9) - 3x$

43   0-88012-866-6

Solving Addition Equations

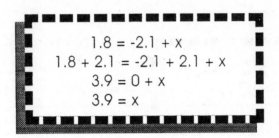

$$1.8 = -2.1 + x$$
$$1.8 + 2.1 = -2.1 + 2.1 + x$$
$$3.9 = 0 + x$$
$$3.9 = x$$

1. $a + -7 = 8$

2. $y + 76 = -93$

3. $4 + b = -14$

4. $-33 = z + 16$

5. $-12 + x = 21$

6. $2.4 = m + 3.7$

7. $-1\dfrac{1}{2} + n = -1\dfrac{5}{8}$

8. $-27 = c + 27$

9. $-\dfrac{5}{8} + x = -\dfrac{5}{8}$

10. $y + -6.2 = 8.1$

0-88012-866-6

Solving Subtraction Equations

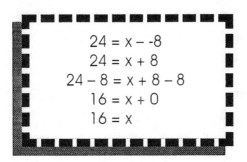

$$24 = x - \text{-}8$$
$$24 = x + 8$$
$$24 - 8 = x + 8 - 8$$
$$16 = x + 0$$
$$16 = x$$

1. $k - 36 = 37$

2. $-22 = y - 8$

3. $x - \text{-}7 = \text{-}19$

4. $30 = b - \text{-}2$

5. $a - 18 = \text{-}32$

6. $-1.7 = b - 9.3$

7. $-4\dfrac{1}{3} = q - 3\dfrac{1}{3}$

8. $-17 = a - 17$

9. $p - \dfrac{3}{5} = \dfrac{3}{5}$

10. $5.62 = m - 6$

Solving Multiplication Equations

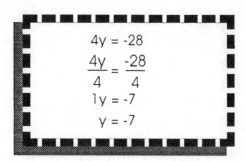

$$4y = -28$$
$$\frac{4y}{4} = \frac{-28}{4}$$
$$1y = -7$$
$$y = -7$$

1. $-6a = -66$

2. $-180 = 12b$

3. $-13n = 13$

4. $42 = -14p$

5. $1\frac{1}{2} = 3x$

6. $-5.6 = -.8x$

7. $8 = -32b$

8. $9a = -3$

9. $.25y = 1.5$

10. $-.0006 = .02x$

       0-88012-866-6

Solving Division Equations

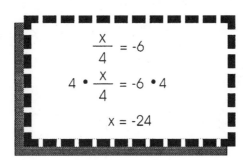

$$\frac{x}{4} = -6$$

$$4 \cdot \frac{x}{4} = -6 \cdot 4$$

$$x = -24$$

1. $-18 = \frac{a}{6}$

6. $35 = \frac{x}{-7}$

2. $\frac{x}{6} = -6$

7. $.12 = \frac{y}{.12}$

3. $\frac{y}{-2} = 231$

8. $3 = -\frac{1}{8}a$

4. $\frac{1}{5}b = -8$

9. $\frac{w}{-2} = .04$

5. $\frac{m}{.6} = .3$

10. $\frac{u}{-4} = -14$

Mixed Practice with Equations

1. $x + 12 = 8$

2. $\dfrac{y}{-6} = 2$

3. $-10 = m - 6$

4. $2.7 = 3y$

5. $-1 = \dfrac{r}{20}$

6. $15 + a = -8$

7. $-7b = -84$

8. $-23 + w = 48$

9. $9 = 54m$

10. $\dfrac{1}{16}x = 8$

11. $-42 = y - 20$

12. $92 + x = 92$

13. $2.5 = \dfrac{a}{.5}$

14. $-84 = 58 + a$

0-88012-866-6

Solving Equations with 2 Operations

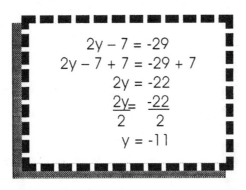

$$2y - 7 = -29$$
$$2y - 7 + 7 = -29 + 7$$
$$2y = -22$$
$$\frac{2y}{2} = \frac{-22}{2}$$
$$y = -11$$

1. $13 + -3p = -2$

5. $-10 + \dfrac{a}{4} = 9$

2. $\dfrac{-5a}{2} = 75$

6. $17 = 5 - x$

3. $6x - 4 = -10$

7. $-7r - 8 = -14$

4. $9 = 2y + 9$

8. $\dfrac{4y}{-3} = 8$

0-88012-866-6

Solving Equations with Negative Variables

$$\frac{-k}{6} + 1 = -5$$

$$\frac{-k}{6} + 1 - 1 = -5 - 1$$

$$\frac{-k}{6} = -6$$

$$-6 \cdot \frac{-k}{6} = -6 \cdot -6$$

$$k = 36$$

1. $-8 - y = 22$

2. $18 = -k + 3$

3. $4 - \dfrac{x}{5} = -16$

4. $-x - 15 = -15$

5. $-z = 11$

6. $-28 = \dfrac{-y}{4} - 12$

7. $-82 = -a$

8. $\dfrac{-b}{3} + 50 = 100$

0-88012-866-6

Solving Equations Using the Distributive Property

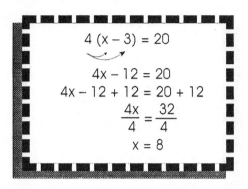

$4 (x - 3) = 20$

$4x - 12 = 20$

$4x - 12 + 12 = 20 + 12$

$\dfrac{4x}{4} = \dfrac{32}{4}$

$x = 8$

1. $3 (x + 8) = -6$

5. $17 (x - 2) = -34$

2. $75 = -5 (a + 5)$

6. $63 = 9 (2 - a)$

3. $-8 (y - 6) = -16$

7. $6 (2 - \dfrac{x}{6}) = 1$

4. $20 = 4 (\dfrac{t}{4} - 2)$

8. $-54 = 3 (2 + 5m)$

Solving Equations — Variables on Both Sides

$$5x + 6 = 2x + 15$$
$$5x - 2x + 6 = 2x - 2x + 15$$
$$3x + 6 = 15$$
$$3x + 6 - 6 = 15 - 6$$
$$\frac{3x}{3} = \frac{9}{3}$$
$$x = 3$$

1. $20y + 5 = 5y + 65$

2. $13 - t = t - 7$

3. $-3k + 10 = k + 2$

4. $-9r = 20 + r$

5. $6m - 2\frac{1}{2} = m + 12\frac{1}{2}$

6. $18 + 4.5p = 6p + 12$

7. $5x - \frac{1}{4} = 3x - \frac{5}{4}$

8. $-x - 2 = 1 - 2x$

Keep in mind...
Tackle all your problems by taking them
one at a time.

Writing Algebraic Expressions

The product of four and 11	$4 \cdot 11$
A number increased by six	$x + 6$
The number divided by two	$y \div 2$ or $\frac{y}{2}$
Twice a number decreased by one	$2a - 1$

1. Five less than a number

2. Three times the sum of a number and twelve

3. Ten more than the quotient of c and three

4. Two increased by six times a number

5. Two-thirds of a number minus eleven

6. Twice the difference between c and four

7. The product of nine and a number, decreased by seven

8. Six times a number plus seven times the number

0-88012-866-6

Solving Problems...

Nine more than a number is 33.
Find the number.
$$9 + n = 33$$
$$9 - 9 + n = 33 - 9$$
$$n = 24$$

1. A number decreased by 16 is -26. Find the number.

2. One fourth of a number is -60. Find the number.

3. The product of negative eight and a number is 104. Find the number.

4. Tim weighs five pounds more than Mitchell. Find Mitchell's weight if Tim weighs ninety-three pounds.

5. The cost of five books is $71.00. What is the cost of each book?

54 0-88012-866-6

... More Problems

> Ten more than 4 times a number is 6.
> What is the number?
> $$10 + 4n = 6$$
> $$10 - 10 + 4n = 6 - 10$$
> $$\frac{4n}{4} = \frac{-4}{4}$$
> $$n = -1$$

1. Three-fifths of a number decreased by one is twenty-three. What is the number?

2. Seven more than six times a number is negative forty-seven. What is the number?

3. Nine less than twice a number is thirty-one. What is the number?

4. Carol is sixty-six inches tall. This is twenty inches less than two times Mindy's height. How tall is Mindy?

5. In February, Paul's electric bill was three dollars more than one-half his gas bill. If the electric bill was ninety-two dollars, what was the gas bill?

Problem Solving

...And More Problems

One number is seven times a second number. Their sum is 112. Find the numbers.

$$n + 7n = 112$$
$$\frac{8n}{8} = \frac{112}{8}$$
$$n = 14 \text{ and } 98$$

1. One of two numbers is five more than the other. The sum of the numbers is 17. Find the numbers.

2. The difference of two numbers is 19. The larger number is 3 more than twice the smaller. Find the numbers.

3. 320 tickets were sold to the school play. There were 3 times as many student tickets sold as adult tickets. Find the number of each.

4. The first number is eight more than the second number. Three times the second number plus twice the first number is equal to 26. Find the numbers.

5. Dan has five times as many $1 bills as $5 bills. He has a total of 48 bills. How many of each does he have?

© 2006 Frank Schaffer Publications   0-88012-866-6

... And Still More Problems

Five times a number equals sixteen less than three times the number. Find the number.

$$5n = 3n - 16$$
$$5n - 3n = 3n - 3n - 16$$
$$\frac{2n}{2} = \frac{-16}{2}$$
$$n = -8$$

1. Twenty decreased by twice a number is ten less than three times the number. Find the number.

2. Half of a number is 18 more than five times the number. Find the number.

3. The length of a rectangle is 4 feet more than twice the width. Five times the width is the same as twice the length increased by 10 feet. Find the dimensions.

4. Mike is 5 years older than David. Four times David's age increased by three years equals three times Mike's age decreased by two years. Find Mike's age.

5. One board is one-third the length of another. Six times the sum of the length of the short board and -10 is equal to the length of the longer board decreased by 11 inches. Find the length of the longer board.

Inequalities

 Keep in mind...
You only fail when you stop trying.

Number Lines

Graph each inequality using a number line.

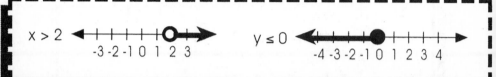

$x > 2$ -3 -2 -1 0 1 2 3 $y \leq 0$ -4 -3 -2 -1 0 1 2 3 4

1. $x > 1$

    -5 -4 -3 -2 -1 0 1 2 3 4 5

2. $a < -1$

    -5 -4 -3 -2 -1 0 1 2 3 4 5

3. $y \leq 2$

    -5 -4 -3 -2 -1 0 1 2 3 4 5

4. $b > -4$

    -5 -4 -3 -2 -1 0 1 2 3 4 5

5. $p \geq 3$

    -5 -4 -3 -2 -1 0 1 2 3 4 5

6. $x < \dfrac{1}{2}$

    -5 -4 -3 -2 -1 0 1 2 3 4 5

7. $y > -1.5$

    -5 -4 -3 -2 -1 0 1 2 3 4 5

8. $m \leq 4\dfrac{1}{2}$

    -5 -4 -3 -2 -1 0 1 2 3 4 5

Solving Inequalities with Addition or Subtraction

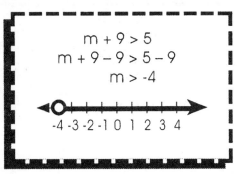

$$m + 9 > 5$$
$$m + 9 - 9 > 5 - 9$$
$$m > -4$$

1. $g + 8 > 6$

5. $-4 \leq 1 + c$

2. $d - 7 > -3$

6. $x + \dfrac{1}{4} \geq 1\dfrac{1}{2}$

3. $-3 > y + 1$

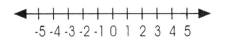

7. $-2.4 < n - .6$

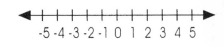

4. $a - 3 \leq 1$

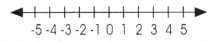

8. $-20 + m \leq -24$

0-88012-866-6

Solving Inequalities with Multiplication or Division

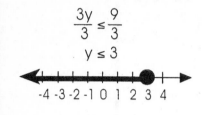

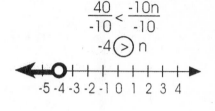

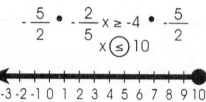

Note: division or multiplication by a negative.

1. $11x > 22$

2. $-15m \leq -75$

3. $-1 > \dfrac{b}{3}$

4. $1.9x \leq -7.6$

5. $\dfrac{3}{2} y < 6$

6. $-26m \geq 13$

7. $-4 \geq \dfrac{2}{3} x$

8. $-2c < 2$

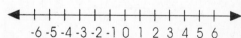

 0-88012-866-6

Solving Inequalities with More Than One Operation

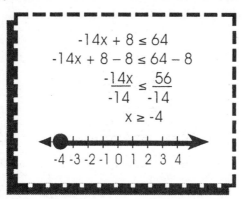

$$-14x + 8 \leq 64$$
$$-14x + 8 - 8 \leq 64 - 8$$
$$\frac{-14x}{-14} \leq \frac{56}{-14}$$
$$x \geq -4$$

1. $7x - 1 < 20$

2. $-4 + 2z \geq -8$

3. $-6x - 9 \geq -3$

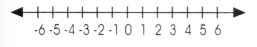

4. $4(2b - 3) \geq 36$

5. $7 < 5x - 8$

6. $-17 > -7x - 45$

7. $-5(2t - 1) \leq 5$

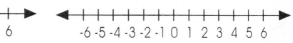

8. $8 - 4x > -12$

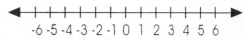

0-88012-866-6

Solving Inequalities with Variables on Both Sides

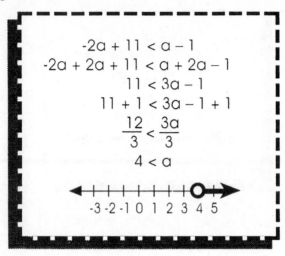

$$-2a + 11 < a - 1$$
$$-2a + 2a + 11 < a + 2a - 1$$
$$11 < 3a - 1$$
$$11 + 1 < 3a - 1 + 1$$
$$\frac{12}{3} < \frac{3a}{3}$$
$$4 < a$$

1. $4c + 1 < -(5 + 2c)$

2. $2 - n > 2n + 11$

3. $2(3x - 5) > 2x + 6$

4. $-2(4y - 21) \leq 12y - 16 + 9y$

5. $n - 3n \geq -4n - 7$

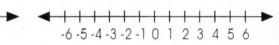

6. $10(x + 2) > -2(6 - 9x)$

7. $11 + 3(-8 + 5x) < 16x - 8$

8. $12(2x + 3) \geq 3(9 + 7x)$

 0-88012-866-6

Mixed Practice with Inequalities

1. $9x - 8 + x < 16 + 4x$

```
-7 -6 -5 -4 -3 -2 -1 0 1 2 3 4 5 6 7
```

2. $15y \geq -45$

```
-7 -6 -5 -4 -3 -2 -1 0 1 2 3 4 5 6 7
```

3. $69 > c + 71$

```
-7 -6 -5 -4 -3 -2 -1 0 1 2 3 4 5 6 7
```

4. $17 + 11n - 13 \leq 4(n + 1) + 2n$

```
-7 -6 -5 -4 -3 -2 -1 0 1 2 3 4 5 6 7
```

5. $8(2 + x) > 3(x - 3)$

```
-7 -6 -5 -4 -3 -2 -1 0 1 2 3 4 5 6 7
```

6. $-4(3x + 2) \geq 40$

```
-7 -6 -5 -4 -3 -2 -1 0 1 2 3 4 5 6 7
```

7. $\dfrac{5}{3} < \dfrac{2}{3}x - 1$

```
-7 -6 -5 -4 -3 -2 -1 0 1 2 3 4 5 6 7
```

8. $3n - 4(2n - 5) + n + 4 \geq 0$

```
-7 -6 -5 -4 -3 -2 -1 0 1 2 3 4 5 6 7
```

A Logical Conclusion

Mike, Dale, Paul and Charlie are the athletic director, quarterback, pitcher and goalie, but not necessarily in that order. From these five statements, identify the man in each position.

1. Mike and Dale were both at the ball park when the rookie pitcher played his first game.

2. Both Paul and the athletic director had played on the same team in high school with the goalie.

3. The athletic director, who scouted Charlie, is planning to watch Mike during his next game.

4. Mike doesn't know Dale.

5. One of these men is a quarterback.

	Quarterback	Goalie	Pitcher	Athletic Director
Mike				
Dale				
Paul				
Charlie				

 0-88012-866-6

Ordered Pairs and Graphing

 Keep in mind...
Challenges make you discover things about yourself
that you never really knew.

— Cicely Tyson

Plotting Points

Connect each of the following ordered pairs.

$(x, y) = (0, -1)$ ⎯⎯ vertical move ⟹ down one

⎯⎯ horizontal move ⟹ no move

"Ancient History"

Start at (0, -1)

(1, -1)	(0, 3)
(1, -3)	(-1, 4)
(3, -3)	(-2, 3)
(3, -1)	(-3, 4)
(5, 0)	(-4, 3)
(8, 0)	(-5, 1)
(7, 1)	(-8, 2)
(9, 0)	(-5, 0)
(8, 2)	(-3, -1)
(5, 1)	(-3, -3)
(4, 3)	(-1, -3)
(3, 4)	(-1, -1)
(2, 3)	(0, -1)
(1, 4)	End

 0-88012-866-6

Coordinates and Graphing

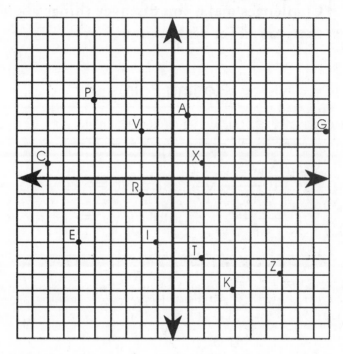

Find the coordinates associated with the following points.

1. A

2. K

3. E

4. P

5. T

6. C

Find the letter associated with each pair of coordinates.

7. (2, 1)

8. (-1, -4)

9. (10, 3)

10. (7, -6)

11. (-2, -1)

12. (-2, 3)

 0-88012-866-6

Solving for y

Solve each equation for y. Then use the given values for x to find the corresponding values for y. Write answers as ordered pairs.

$$y - 4 = 3x \qquad \text{Let } x = -2, 0, 1$$
$$y - 4 + 4 = 3x + 4$$
$$y = 3x + 4 \qquad \Big\}\text{ Solve for y}$$

a. $y = 3 \bullet -2 + 4$ b. $y = 3 \bullet 0 + 4$ c. $y = 3 \bullet 1 + 4$
    $y = -6 + 4$ $y = 0 + 4$ $y = 3 + 4$
    $y = -2$ $y = 4$ $y = 7$
    $(-2, -2)$ $(0, 4)$ $(1, 7)$

1. $y = 5x$ Let $x = -3, 0, 2$ Note: This equation is already in the form of y = ...

2. $2x + y = 9$ Let $x = -1, 0, 5$

3. $-x = y + 3$ Let $x = -3, 0, 4$

4. $y = \dfrac{2}{3}x + 1$ Let $x = -4, 0, 3$

5. $8x + y = 1$ Let $x = -2, 0, 1$

Graphing Linear Equations by Plotting Points

Solve each equation for y. Then choose 3 values for x and find the corresponding values for y. Graph the 3 ordered pairs and draw the line that contains them.

$$5x + y = -1$$
$$5x - 5x + y = -1 - 5x$$
$$y = -5x - 1$$

x	y
-1	4
0	-1
2	-11

a. $y = -5 \cdot -1 - 1$
   $y = 5 - 1$
   $y = 4$

b. $y = -5 \cdot 0 - 1$
   $y = 0 - 1$
   $y = -1$

c. $y = -5 \cdot 2 - 1$
   $y = -10 - 1$
   $y = -11$

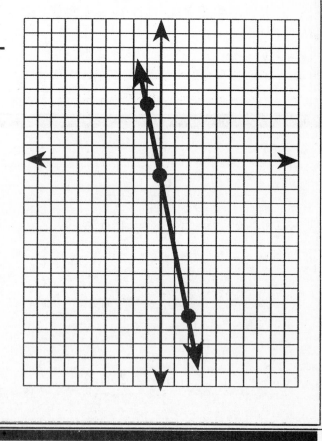

0-88012-866-6

1. $-3x + y = -4$

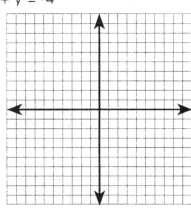

4. $\frac{1}{4}x + y = -2$

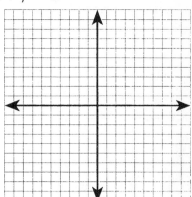

2. $y - x = -1$

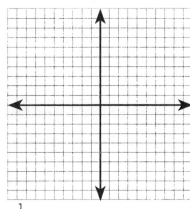

5. $y = -4x - 5$

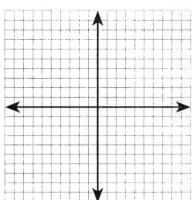

3. $y = -\frac{1}{2}x$

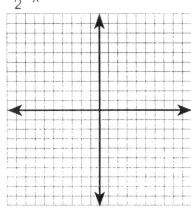

6. $y = -2x - 3$

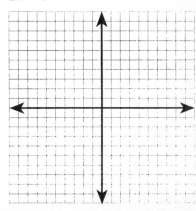

0-88012-866-6

Slope

Find the slope of the line passing through the given points.

I. Using the graph of the line

$$\text{slope} = \frac{\text{change in y}}{\text{change in x}}$$

Choose any 2 points to count the change.

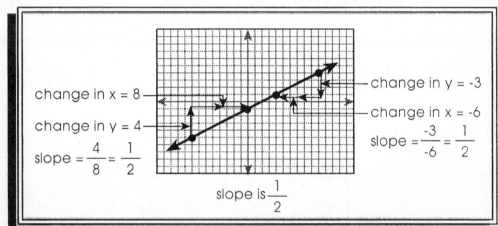

change in x = 8

change in y = 4

$\text{slope} = \frac{4}{8} = \frac{1}{2}$

change in y = -3

change in x = -6

$\text{slope} = \frac{-3}{-6} = \frac{1}{2}$

slope is $\frac{1}{2}$

1.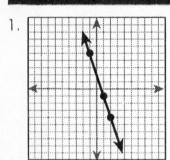

2.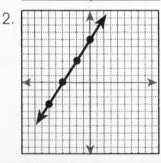

3.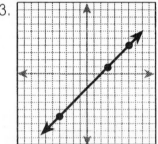

4.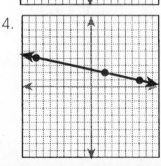

...More Slope

II. Using the formula

$$\text{slope} = \frac{\text{difference in y-values}}{\text{difference in x-values}}$$

P (5, 3)   R (-1, 1)

$$\text{slope of PR} = \frac{3-1}{5-(-1)} = \frac{2}{6} = \frac{1}{3}$$

$$\text{slope is } \frac{1}{3}$$

1. A (-3, 1)   D (4, 5)   6. Q (0, -4)   R (1, -6)

2. C (2, 6)   F (3, 5)   7. L (-2, 6)   N (2, -3)

3. B (0, 8)   G (3, 2)   8. S (-1, -3)   X (2, -6)

4. J (-6, -3)   K (-4, 5)   9. T (-4, -4)   Z (6, 3)

5. P (9, 4)   M (7, 3)   10. V $(\frac{3}{4}, \frac{3}{2})$ W $(\frac{11}{4}, \frac{5}{2})$

       0-88012-866-6

Ordered Pairs and Graphing

Graphing Linear Equations Using Slope

Graph the line that contains the given point and has the given slope.

$(2, -1), \dfrac{2}{3}$

a. Plot point.
b. Locate other points by moving up 2 units and to the right 3 units.
c. Connect the points with a line.

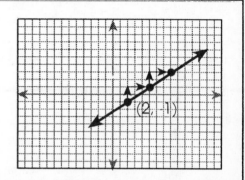

1. $(-5, -2), -\dfrac{1}{2}$

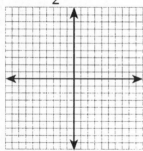

3. $(2, -3), \dfrac{3}{4}$

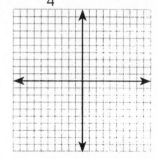

2. $(4, 2), 3$ (note: $3 = \dfrac{3}{1}$)

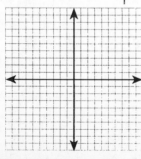

4. $(0, 2), -\dfrac{5}{2}$

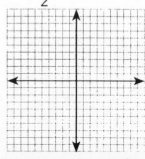

0-88012-866-6